SCHIRMER'S LIBRARY OF MUSICAL CLASSICS

Vol. 2066

FIRST LESSONS IN BACH

COMPLETE
Books I and II

For the Piano

Compiled and Fingered by Walter Carroll

ISBN-13: 978-1-4234-2192-4

G. SCHIRMER, Inc.

DISTRIBUTED BY
HAL•LEONARD®
CORPORATION
7777 W. BLUEMOUND RD. P.O. BOX 13819 MILWAUKEE, WI 53213

PREFACE

The appreciation of Bach as a tremendous force in the progress of music has been growing steadily since the early 20th century. The performance of his incomparable works, whose influence flows in an ever widening channel through the whole domain of musical education, has clearly demonstrated that the practical study of Bach is the gateway to the mastery of technique. It has accomplished still more; for out of the *knowledge* of Bach has grown the *love* of Bach, and the love of Bach has helped materially in creating that taste for good music which is so striking a feature of the present and so hopeful a sign for the future.

Bach wrote a large number of charming little pieces which provide elementary teaching material of priceless value. Short, melodious, and rhythmical, they are played with keen delight by young pupils in the early years of their instruction and serve as a natural stepping-stone to the vast store of intermediate and advanced compositions of the same writer. All the movements contain features of real educational worth which will repay special attention and care. Each number should pass through three stages of preparation: — (a) Accuracy of notes, time, and fingering. (b) Closer attention to phrasing, expression, and speed. (c) Performance from memory. Whether they be used as studies or as pieces is immaterial, as they combine the technical value of the one with the grace and charm of the other. Any pupil capable of playing a very easy sonatina may commence the regular study of Bach and thus early learn to love, in simple for, those elements of truth, sincerity, and refinement which are revealed in every bar of his music; elements at once the source of his greatness and the measure of his power.

Book I is compiled with the object of placing within reach of the teacher a series of very easy pieces in convenient form. With the exception of Nos. 6, 7, 8, 12, and 15, all the pieces in Book I are from the *Notebook for Anna Magdalena Bach*, the composer's second wife.

Book II is intended to serve as a link between Book I and the *Little Preludes* or the *Two-part Inventions*. The pieces are selected from the following works:—Nos. 1, 3, and 6 from the *Notebook for Anna Magdalena Bach*; Nos. 2, 4, and 10 from the *English Suites*; Nos. 7, 8, and 11 from the *French Suites*; No. 5 from an Overture; No. 9 from a Partita; No. 12 from a Suite.

Regular and systematic study of the works contained in "First Lessons" will awaken, early in the pupil's training, a genuine desire for good music and an interest in the music of Bach which, when once aroused, is the surest and the quickest means of developing technique and expression in piano playing.

—Walter Carroll

CONTENTS

FIRST LESSONS IN BACH

BOOK I

1. Minuet

A study in accent and in the correct timing of half-beats.

2. Minuet

A study in accent and in obtaining a proper balance of tone.

(At the close of this movement the previous Minuet may be repeated)

3. Minuet

A study in the arpeggio of the Common Chord (close position).

4. Polonaise

A study in phrasing and in the correct timing of quarter-beats.

(At the close of this movement Minuet No. 3 may be repeated)

5. March

A study in syncopation and in keeping a steady beat throughout.

6. Minuet

A study in contrasting rhythmic patterns between the hands.

(Nos. 6, 7, 8, after being studied separately, may be grouped together for performance in the order 7, 6, 8)

7. Minuet

A study in legato playing, with careful balance of tone.

8. Minuet

A study in tone-values, the lower part to be slightly more prominent than the upper.
(Compare with No. 7)

14

9. March

A study in staccato touch, repeated notes and observance of rests.

10. Minuet

A study in phrasing, legato touch and balance of tone.

11. Musette

A study in sustained notes and quality of tone.

12. Bourrée

A study in contrasts of touch and independence of each hand.

13. Musette

A study in broken octaves and in neat phrasing.

Allegro con brio ♩ = 112

14. Minuet

A study in expression, phrasing and beauty of tone.

15. Gavotte

A study in phrasing, gradation of tone and cantabile playing.

16. March

A study in the accurate timing of triplets and in steadiness of rhythm.

FIRST LESSONS IN BACH

BOOK II

Polonaise

A study in accuracy of rhythm and in neatness of phrasing

Gavotte

A study in accompaniment touch

Andante pastorale ($\quad$ = 112)

Polonaise

A study in contrasts of tone and in clearness of melody

Gavotte

A study in legato touch and independence of each hand

Minuet

A study in phrasing and in balance of tone

Polonaise

A study in staccato and in elementary part-playing

Gavotte

A study in contrasts of touch and in clearness of outline

Minuet

A study in evenness of touch and in beauty of tone

Scherzo

A study in contrasts of touch and independence of each hand

Sarabande

A study in expression and in balance of parts

Andante con espressione (♩ = 84)

Minuet

A study in phrasing and in quality of tone

36

Prelude

A study in part-playing and in the use of the inverted mordent

Moderato ♩= 92

12.